Two in One:
Excel and Access 2016 for Beginners

Two in One:
Excel and Access 2016 for Beginners
Ali Akbar

Kanzul Ilmi Press
2017

First Printing: 2017

Editor: Zico Pratama Putra

Kanzul Ilmi Press
Woodside Ave.
London, UK

Bookstores and wholesalers: Please contact Kanzul Ilmi Press email

zico.pratama@gmail.com.

Trademark Acknowledgments

All terms mentioned in this book that is known to be trademarks or service marks have been appropriately capitalized. Microsoft, Inc., cannot attest to the accuracy of this information. Use of a term in this book should not be regarded as affecting the validity of any trademark or service mark.

Ms. Excel and Ms. Access are registered trademark of Microsoft, Inc.

Unless otherwise indicated herein, any the third-party trademarks that may appear in this work are the property of their respective owners and any references to the third-party trademark, logos or other trade dress are for demonstrative or descriptive purposes only

Ordering Information: Special discounts are available on quantity purchases by corporations, associations, educators, and others. For details, contact the publisher at the above-listed address.

CHAPTER 1 CONTENTS

Chapter 1 LEARNING EXCEL

Microsoft Excel and Access are two primary software in MS Office package. Microsoft. Excel is used to do spreadsheet analysis and Access is used to do some relational database data operation. This two software can be used to help any of your office needs.

Pic 1.1 Excel and Access, two most important software in MS Office

1.1   Introduction to Excel

Microsoft Excel is the most important and most famous spreadsheet app used in businesses and offices around the world. Excel can be used as a spreadsheet calculator for every type of business. This is a universal spreadsheet app that is quickly learned.

An excel app, has many features, such as calculations and graphics creations. Since this program is straightforward to be learned, Excel becomes the most popular spreadsheet app today.

MS Excel used on many platforms, such as windows, or Macintosh. Excel already released on MacOC Since version 5.0 on 1993.

Right now, MS Excel is an integral part of Microsoft Office package.

Pic 1.2 Office 2016 logo

1.1.1 Running Excel

Running excel can be done using many techniques. If you use Win 8 or above, click Start > All Programs > Microsoft Office then click Excel. Or you may use **Run** window by clicking Windows + R then type and execute "excel" command.

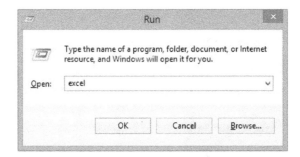

Pic 1.3 Typing "excel" command to run MS Excel

A splash screen will emerge:

Pic 1.4 Splash screen excel 2016

1.1.2 Creating Workbook

The workbook is an excel file. This can be used to save all information you need. To be able to perform a spreadsheet calculation, you need to create a workbook first.

Here are steps you can do to create a workbook:

1. After excel window shown, click on the Blank Workbook:

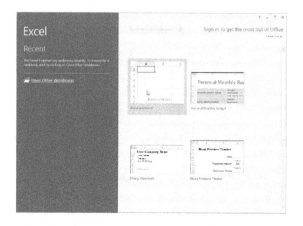

Pic 1.5 Click on the Blank Workbook to create workbook

2. An empty workbook will be set up but hasn't yet saved. You will do spreadsheet calculation here.

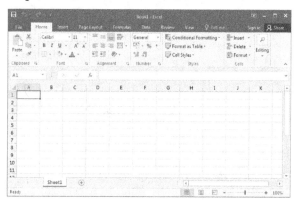

Pic 1.6 Excel 2016 workbook interface

1.1.3 Introduction to the Excel's Interfaces

To be able to work with excel, you have to know first, the functions of buttons and other interfaces of Excel.

1.1.3.1 Quick Access Toolbar

Quick Access Toolbar is a toolbar on the top left of your excel app. You can access commands quickly using this toolbar because you don't have to open ribbon tabs. On its initial condition, Quick Access Toolbar only have three buttons, Save, Undo, and Repeat.

Pic 1.7 Quick access toolbar

But you can also add other buttons or commands to make your access to those buttons faster. Here are steps you can do to add buttons to quick access toolbar:

1. Click on the arrow icon on the right side of quick access toolbar.

Pic 1.8 Menu to Customize Quick Access Toolbar

2. Choose command button you want to add. To select other commands, click **More Commands**.

Pic 1.9 Menu to insert new button to quick access toolbar

3. If it's already inserted and has a checked sign, the command button will add to quick access toolbar.

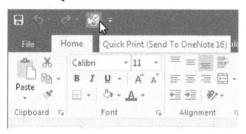

Pic 1.10 new button already added to Quick Access Toolbar

1.1.3.2 Name box

Name box will display selected cell's name. If you choose a range (more than one cells), this will show range's identity. For example, if cell B4 is being selected, name box will display "B4", that shows the selected column is B and selected row is 4.

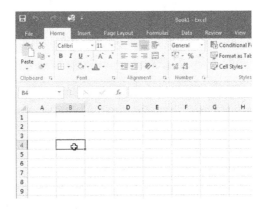

Pic 1.11 When name box display "B4".

1.1.3.3 Formula Bar

You can insert data, or edit data using formula bar. For example, when cell B2 entered "2016" you will find formula bar like this.

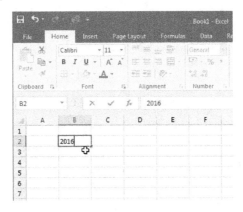

Pic 1.12 Formula bar when a user enters a content to cell B2.

1.1.3.4 Ribbons

Ribbons contain all commands needed to perform calculations, formatting, etc. Ribbons have many ribbons dedicated to each function, such as Home, Insert, Page Layout, etc. Just click the tab of the ribbon, it'll display the buttons inside the ribbon.

Pic 1.13 Ribbon in Excel

1.1.3.5 Column

The column is the vertical part of the cell. In Excel, column identified by alphabets, such as A, B, C and so forth.

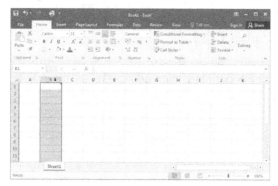

Pic 1.14 Column B selected

1.1.3.6 Row

The row is the horizontal part. You can choose a row on its left. In excel, row identified by a number.

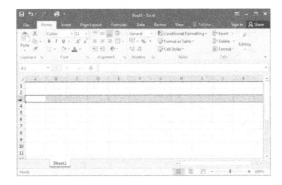

Pic 1.15 Row in excel

1.1.3.7 Worksheet

If excel file is a workbook, then a sheet in excel spreadsheet is called worksheet, A workbook can contain more than one worksheet. When a workbook created, there will be on worksheet created by default. In older version of excel, there are three sheets created.

You can rename, add, and delete worksheets.

1.1.4.8 Horizontal Scroll Bar

Horizontal scrollbar used to scroll worksheet's position on Excel. You can slide the scroll bar or click the right arrow or left arrow button.

Pic 1.16 Scrollbar

1.1.4.9 Zoom Control

The size of spreadsheet display can be zoomed out or zoomed in. You can use this button to do so. Just click and drag zoom slider to make the image larger or smaller. The zoom value can be seen on the right. Standard is 100%, more than 100% means greater, less than 100% means lower.

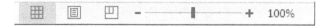

Pic 1.17 Zoom control to control the zoom

1.1.4 Open Workbook

To open a workbook, you can perform steps below:

1. Click File tab.

2. Click Open. You will see the window below:

Pic 1.18 File > Open top menu to open Excel file

3. Choose the file you want to open:

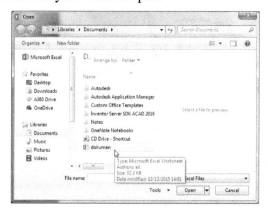

Pic 1.19 Select the file to open

4. You can also open in another place, like OneDrive or in the network.

5. Click the **Open** button, and the file will be opened.

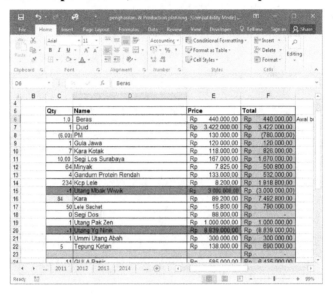

Pic 1.20 Workbook opened

1.1.5 Saving Workbook

If the workbook created already, you can change the content of the workbook and then save the workbook again. Saving means the change you created will be permanently implemented.

To save, you just click CTRL + S shortcut on the keyboard. Or click the Diskette button on quick access toolbar.

Pic 1.21 Diskette icon on quick access toolbar to save workbook

You can also click from File ribbon. Click the File > Save. This will open Save As window if you haven't saved the file before. You can save it into OneDrive, local PC or another place in the network by clicking **Add a Place**.

Pic 1.22 Click Save to save into this PC

1.2 Cell Operations

A cell is an intersection between a row and a column. You can put a value on a cell. You can also create functions, and do some data calculation here.

1.2.1 Modify Column, Row, and Cell

A column has a uniform width, but you can enlarge or constrict column's width. To modify column width, you can do steps below:

1. Put your pointer between column. The pointer will change its icon like below:

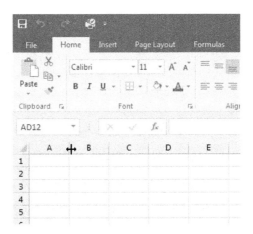

Pic 1.23 Put pointer below

2. Slide right to increase the column's width. The pixel size of the column's width will emerge, you can slide it to match the size you want.

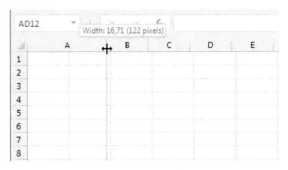

Pic1.24 Click and drag to change the column's width

3. If you release the drag click, the new width of the column will   be   implemented.

Pic 1.25 Column's width after changed

4. If you want to change the column's width precisely using the pixel's number size, then click the column's header, right click and choose **Column Width** menu.

Pic 1.26 Choose Column Width menu

5. Enter the column's width in pixel. Click OK.

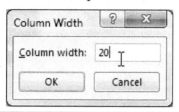

6. The column will change its width according to the pixel value inserted.

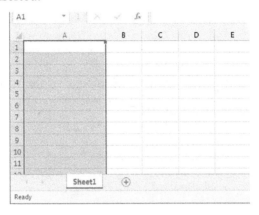

Pic 1.28 Column width after modified by adding the pixel value

For rows, the method is similar. You can do it using steps below:

1. Put the pointer on the border between rows. The pointer will change its icon like this pic below:

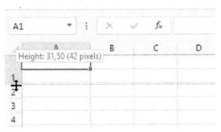

Pic 1.29 Pointer's icon changed

2. Click and drag below to increase the row's size.

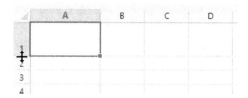

Pic 1.30 Sliding the pointer's icon to resize the row

3. If you want to enter the new pixel size of the row, just click row's header on the left, then click **Row height** menu.

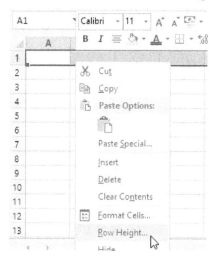

Pi c1.31 Right-click and choose Row height menu

4. Insert the new row height value in the pixel, and click **OK**.

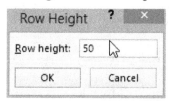

Pic 1.32 Inserting the new row height value in pixel

5. The row's size will be updated.

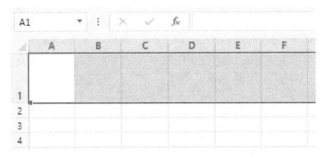

Pic 1.33 Row's height updated

1.2.2 Formatting Cell

The content of a cell can be formatted using these techniques:

1. For example, the cell B4 has a regular number like the pic below; we'll format it.

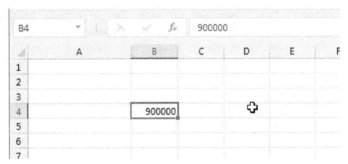

Pic 1.34 Cell B3 that will be formatted

2. Right-click on the cell, and choose **Format Cells** menu.

Pic 1.35 Click on Format Cells menu

3. Because the data type of the cell's content is a number, a Number tab will appear. On Number tab, you can choose the number's type, whether it will be a general number, currency, etc.

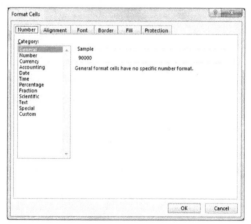

Pic 1.36 Number tab

4. To create a currency, click on Currency on Category box. Then choose a symbol for the currency, and choose the decimals amount needed.

Pic 1.37 Configuring the currency's formatting

5. On Alignment tab, you can set up the text's alignment on the cell. You can also change the degree of orientation of the text by changing the direction of the text on Orientation box, or by entering the degree value on numeric up down box **Degrees**.

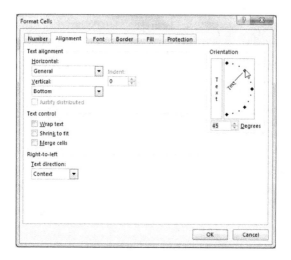

Pic 1.38 Configuring the text orientation

6. Click Font tab to set up the font name, font style, and font size of the text on the cell.

Pic 1.39 Changing the font properties

7. On Border tab, you can create and define edge type and styles. You can choose line type of the edge and which part of cells are bordered.

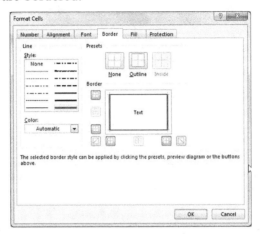

Pic 1.40 Changing border

8. On **Fill** tab, you can modify the background color of the cell. Modify the value on Fill > Background color. You can also implement a pattern by selecting the Pattern Color and Pattern Style combo box.

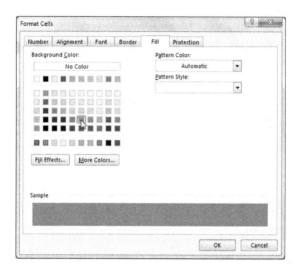

Pic 1.41 Changing Fill properties

9. Click **OK**, the cell and the text inside will be modified according to the selected format.

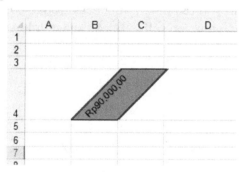

Pic 1.42 Cell and text already changed

1.3   Worksheet Basics

A worksheet is a place where data calculation is performed. There are some basic spreadsheet operations you have to understand.

1.3.1 Add Worksheet

The new worksheet can be added using steps below:

1. Look at the plus sign below the Excel window, right on the worksheet's name. Click on that plus sign.

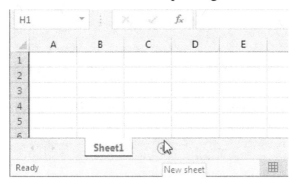

Pic 1.43 Click on plus button to add new worksheet

2. A new sheet will emerge with the default name Sheet(Before+1).

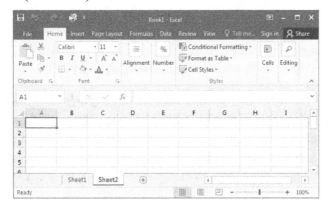

Pic 1.44 New sheet emerge

3. You can also use right click method to create a new sheet, right-click on the sheet's tab and click **Insert**.

Pic 1.45 Clicking the Insert menu to add new worksheet

4. An Insert window will emerge, choose the new type of sheet you want to add.

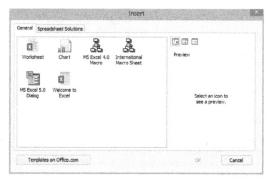

Pic 1.46 Select the new type of sheet

5. You can also create new sheet from existing templates just click the Spreadsheet solutions and click OK. Lots of templates available, such as sales report, billing statement, etc. You can see the preview in Preview box.

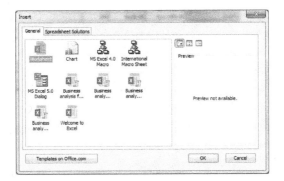

Pic 1.47 Insert template

6. If you create new sheet from a template, the newly created sheet will have some data inside. You can edit or delete this data if you need it.

Pic 1.48 New sheet created with template will have data inside it

1.3.2 Delete Worksheet

The worksheet can be deleted from the workbook. Here is how to delete existing worksheet:

1. Right-click on the sheet's tab you want to delete.

2. Click   on   **Delete**   menu   to   delete   it.

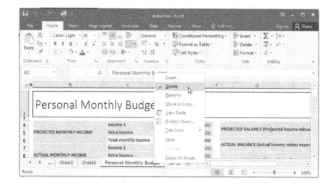

Pic 1.49 Click on Delete menu to delete a sheet

3. The sheet that is removed will be no longer accessible.

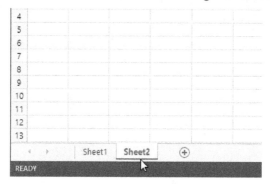

Pic 1.50 Sheets tab after deletion

1.3.3 Change the Sheets Order

Sheets inserted into the workbook will have order according to the time it's inserted. But you can change the sheet's order by drag and drop.

1. For example the initial condition like this, we want to change the Sheet1 position after Sheet2.

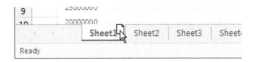

Pic 1.51 Initial sheets order

2. Click on Sheet1 then drag right after the Sheet2's position.

Pic 1.52 Drag Sheet1 to Sheet 2 position

3. Release the drag click, the sheet1's position will slide to the right of Sheet2's position.

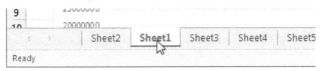

Pic 1.53 Sheet1's position

1.3.4 Rename Sheet

Sheet inserted will have default names like sheet2, sheet3, etc. You can change the sheet's name to make the sheet more readable.

1. To change the sheet's name, double click on sheets' name. The sheet's name will be selected like this:

Pic 1.54 Double click on sheet's name

2. Type the new name.

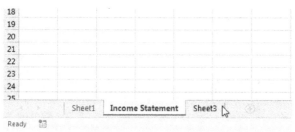

Pic 1.55 Type the new name

3. Click Enter on your keyboard, the new name will be inserted

Pic 1.56 New name will be inserted

4. You can rename from right click menu, just right click on the sheet's name and click **Rename** menu.

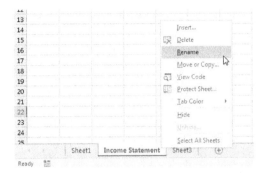

Pic 1.57 Click Rename menu

5. Type the new name. The new name will be implemented.

Pic 1.58 Type new name

1.3.5 Page Layout

Not only can be used as a tool to do spreadsheet calc, but excel can also deliver the result to printed paper. Before you can print, you have to open **Page Layout** tab on the ribbon that accommodates many features of page layout.

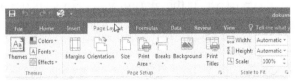

Click Themes and choose a theme you want for your whole spreadsheet. The theme you choose will automatically change the text, color, and font of your worksheet.

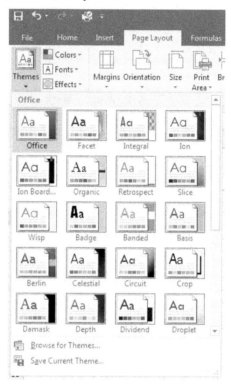

Pic 1.60 Theme list

Click Margins > Custom Margins to configure your margin. The margin is a whitespace between the end of the printed area to the end of the paper. If the margin you choose is not available on the list, you can create your Custom Margin.

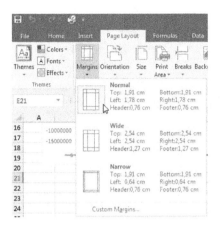

Pic 1.61 Menu to access Custom Margins

Then define the top, right, bottom and left margins. You can set margin for header or footer also.

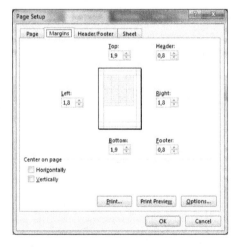

Pic 1.62 Defining custom margin

Paper orientation can be selected between portrait (vertical) or landscape (horizontal).

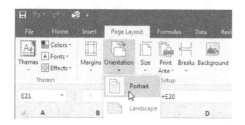

Pic 1.63 Changing paper orientation

To change paper size, click **Size** and choose the paper type.

Pic 1.64 Selecting paper size

Print Area section used to set printing area from the worksheet. Not all worksheet will be printed. You can set certain part of the area   to   be   printable.

Pic 1.65 Set Print Area

Background used to insert background to the worksheet.

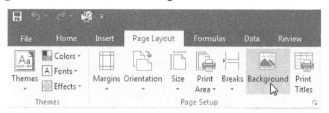

Pic 1.66 Click on Background tab

You can choose image source, from the local file or Bing Image Search. Bing is owned by Microsoft, so MS Office support Bing rather than Google Image Search.

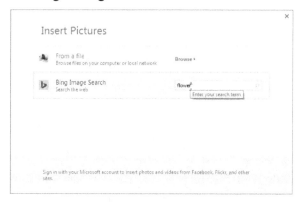

Pic 1.67 Locate image source for worksheet background

Just enter the keyword for your background image search, after that the result will be available in seconds.

Pic 1.68 Images available for background image on Bing Image Search

If you have no internet connection, you can choose local images.

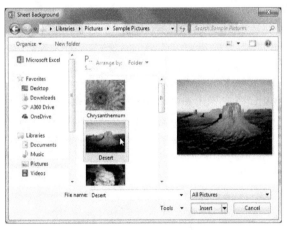

Pic 1.69 Locate image from local computer

After the background image inserted the background are of your worksheet will be no plain anymore.

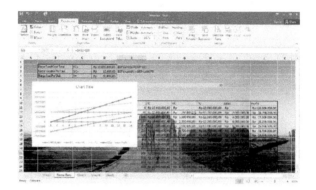

Pic 1.70 Worksheet condition after background image inserted

If you want to delete the background, just click the **Page Layout > Delete Background**.

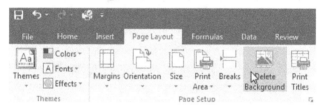

Pic 1.71 Clicking Delete Background button to delete background

If you want to customize the Page Setup, click the arrow on the right bottom side of the Page Setup box in Page Layout ribbon.

Pic 1.72 Button to display Custom Page Setup

A   Page   Setup   window   will   appear:

Pic 1.73 Page Setup window

In Header/Footer tab, you can insert the header and footer for each page in the printed paper. The header is a space on the top of the page, while footer is an area on the bottom of the page.

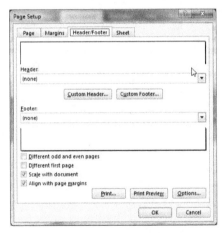

Pic 1.74 Header/Footer tab

1.3.6 Printing Worksheet

Printing in excel is not as simple as in MS Word. You have to define the print area first. It's different with MS Word, where a page in MS Word will appear in a paper if printed directly.

Do steps below to print a worksheet in MS Excel:

1. Select areas (more than one cells) you want to print.

2. Click Page Layout tab. Click **Print Area > Set Print Area**.

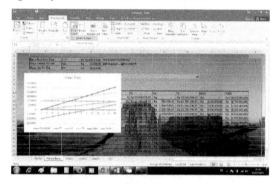

Pic 1.75 Click on Set Print Area button

3. Page Setup > Sheet window will appear. You can see the Print Area selected in text box **Print area**.

Pic 1.76 Print area window

4. Click **File > Print**.

Pic 1.77 Click on File > Print menu

5. You can see the print preview on the right side. You can also configure the printer properties (optional) in Print Properties.

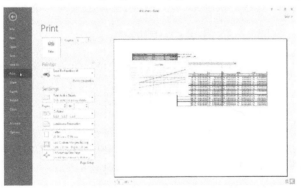

Pic 1.78 Print Preview

6. If everything is OK, then click Print icon to do the print work.

1.4   Excel Formulas

The core of spreadsheet software is formulas. This makes excel is very intelligent and can be used to do many spreadsheet calculations. This is because Excel has the capability to create so many formulas, formula with built-in functions or formula you can define it by yourself.

Excel formulas can be directly used without having to install plug-ins or add-ins first. This is because this function is supported by default in excel.

1.4.1 Create Formulas

All formulas in excel, no matter how complex they are, mainly set up with a simple technique.

1. Click the cell you want to create the formula.

2. Click equal (=) symbol on your keyboard. All equal symbol will tell excel that you will create a formula.

1.4.2 Cell Reference

You can create a formula that gets value from another cell. You just have to reference the other cell to the formula so that the formula can count the value based on the value. This method has many advantages:

1. If the value in other cell changed, the formula will be updated directly and display new value.

2. In certain case, using cell reference, you can copy the formula to another cell (usually adjacent cells) in a worksheet, and the reference in the newly copied will dynamically   update   to   the   cell.

The easiest method to reference cell is using a mouse, just click the cell you want to reference, this will automatically reference the cell into the formula (after the = sign).

1.4.3 Mathematics Formulas

Basic of mathematical formulas are the arithmetical operator, such as multiply, divide, add, and subtract. We'll demonstrate how to use the arithmetical operator in steps below:

1. There is two numerical value we want to operate using excel math formula.

Pic 1.79 Two numerical values will be calculated

2. Enter equal sign to start formula creation.

Pic 1.80 Inserting equal sign to start formula creation

3. Click the first cell that contains the value to operate, or in another word, the first operand.

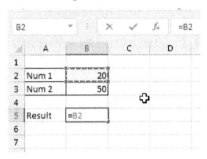

Pic 1.81 Click on the first cell

4. Insert the operator, for this example, I'll use plus operator to perform addition.

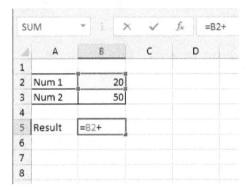

Pic 1.82 Inserting the additional operator

5. Choose the second value as the second operand.

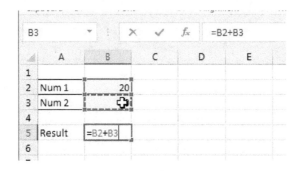

Pic 1.83 Select second value to operate, the second operand

6. Click Enter on your keyboard. This will make the formula inserted. You can see the formula written on the formula bar, and the result of the operation displayed in the cell.

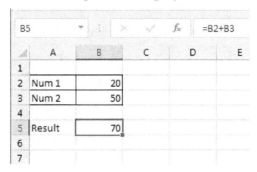

Pic 1.84 Formula already inserted

7. If you click your mouse on the cell again, you will see the formula again.

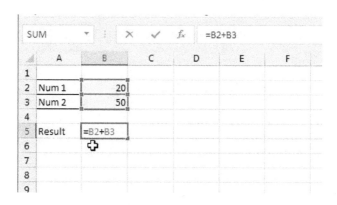

Pic 1.85 Excel formula appeared when you mouse click the cell

8. You can change the operator with * to do multiplication.

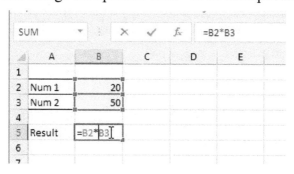

Pic 1.86 Changing the operator to perform multiplication

9. Click Enter, the result of the multiplication will be displayed.

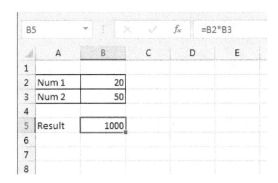

Pic 1.87 Result of the multiplication formula

10. To do division operation, change the operator to type division symbol (/).

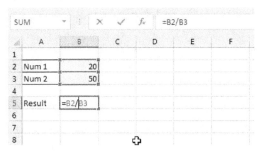

Pic 1.88 Changing the operator to /

11. The result of the formula will be updated in a aftermath of the division.

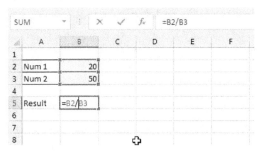

Pic 1.89 The result updated because of division formula

12. To change to subtraction operation, use minus (-) symbol as an operator.

1.90 Minus (-) symbol as operator for subtraction

13. The result will be updated

Pic 1.91 Subtraction result

14. From above steps, you can see those arithmetic operators used in Excel formula are the same with regular mathematics.

Arithmetical operators in Excel have symbols:

1. Subtraction, minus sign (-).

2. Addition, plus sign(+)

3. Division, slash sign (/)

4. Multiplication, asterisk sign (*)

5. Exponential, exponential sign (^)

1.4.4 Named Ranges

The range is a collection more than one cell. To ease the formula creation, you can create a named range. This will make the function more readable. To create named ranges, you could use steps below:

1. For example, there is a table where the second column will be defined as a named range.

	A	B	C	D	E
			C15		
1					
2		Product Sales Report			
3		Temperature	Sales		
4		15	140		
5		14	120		
6		13	140		
7		15	120		
8		14	140		
9		14	200		
10		51	120		
11		21	123		
12		23	130		
13		22	143		
14					
15					
16					
17					
18					

Pic 1.92 Table where the second column will be named

2. Select the range you want to be identified, right click and click **Define Name** menu.

Pic 1.93 Range selected

3. **New Name** window appears, insert the name for this field in the **Name** text box.

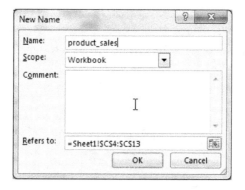

Pic 1.94 Inserting name for selected range

4. When you choose one cell that is a member of the range, the name still unidentified.

C6			×	✓	fx	140	

	A	B	C	D	E
1					
2		Product Sales Report			
3		Temperature	Sales		
4		15	140		
5		14	120		
6		13	140		
7		15	120		
8		14	140		
9		14	200		
10		51	120		
11		21	123		
12		23	130		
13		22	143		
14					
15					
16					

Pic 1.95 If only a cell selected, the name still unidentified

5. But if you choose all the cells of the range, the name will be seen in the top-left text box, adjacent to the formula box.

product_sales			×	✓	fx	140	

	A	B	C	D	E	F
1						
2		Product Sales Report				
3		Temperature	Sales			
4		15	140			
5		14	120			
6		13	140			
7		15	120			
8		14	140			
9		14	200			
10		51	120			
11		21	123			
12		23	130			
13		22	143			
14						
15						
16						

Pic 1.96 Name of the designated range seen on the top left text box

6. Using named range, creating formula easier. Because you can make the formula more readable, for example, you can

just create AVERAGE (named_range) to calculate the mean value from all the cells in the range.

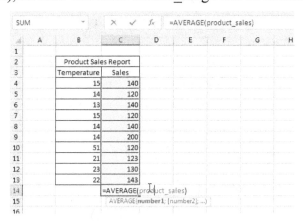

Pic 1.97 Named range used on formula

7. If the named_range's name selected (you put your pointer there), all cells within the named_range will be chosen.

	A	B	C	D	E	F	G	H
1								
2		Product Sales Report						
3		Temperature	Sales					
4		15	140					
5		14	120					
6		13	140					
7		15	120					
8		14	140					
9		14	200					
10		51	120					
11		21	123					
12		23	130					
13		22	143					
14			=AVERAGE(product_sales)					
15			AVERAGE(number1; [number2]; ...)					
16								

SUM — =AVERAGE(product_sales)

Pic 1.98 All cells in named range selected

8. If the formula created, the formula bar will display the formula more readable than just creating using cells address.

C14					f_x	=AVERAGE(product_sales)		
	A	B	C	D	E	F	G	H
1								
2		Product Sales Report						
3		Temperature	Sales					
4		15	140					
5		14	120					
6		13	140					
7		15	120					
8		14	140					
9		14	200					
10		51	120					
11		21	123					
12		23	130					
13		22	143					
14			137,6					
15								

Pic 1.99 Named range

1.5   IF and Logic Functions

To make the formula more advanced, you can use If and other logic functions. This feature will create a logic test to manage the flow of the formula. The value compared using IF and other logic functions is called boolean. Boolean value only has two variations, True or False.

1.5.1 AND

AND will return TRUE only if the two operand has value TRUE. The syntax is:

```
= AND ( operand_1 , operand_2 , ... operand_255 )
```

You can see on steps below:

1. There   are   two   values,   TRUE   and   FALSE.

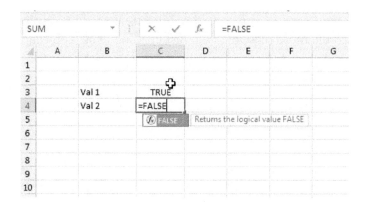

Pic 1.100 Two values TRUE and FALSE as operand

2. Type an equal sign, and use function AND followed by (
then enter the operand, and followed by).

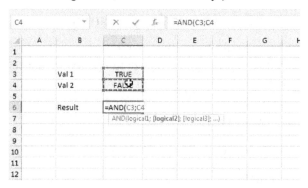

Pic 1.101 Entering AND function and inserting the operand

3. The result is false because one of the operands is false.

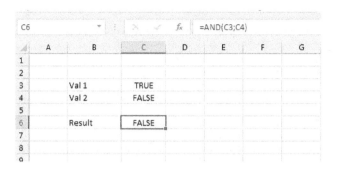

Pic 1.102 Result of the AND function is FALSE

1.5.2 OR

OR function will return a TRUE value if at least one of the operands has value TRUE. The syntax will be like this:

```
= OR ( operand_1 , operand_2 , ... operand_255 )
```

The creation process of this OR function:

1. Enter equal sign = and type "OR" to insert.

2. Choose the range of operands you want to operate using function OR.

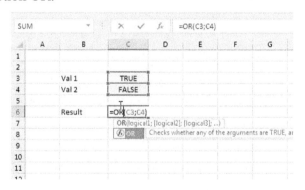

Pic 1.103 Select range of operands to be compared using OR

3. The result of the OR function is True because one of the operands   has   a   True   value.

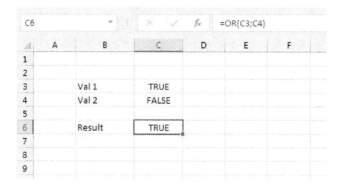

Pic 1.104 Result of OR function

1.5.3 IF

IF function is used for decision-making based on logical value. You can define what action is taken when the if-test valued True and other activities when the if-test valued FALSE.

1. Click on the cell to create a formula using IF function.

2. Enter equal sign to start creating the formula.

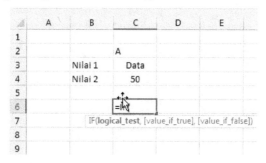

Pic 1.105 Creating Formula with IF function

3. Create the logical test, for example, we want to create whether cell C4's value bigger than 50.

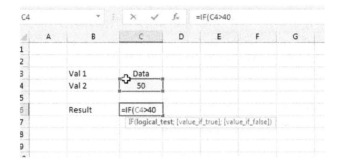

Pic 1.106 Logical test

4. Define text to display when the value True, and text to display if value False.

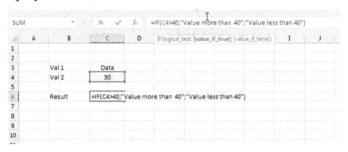

Pic 1.107 Defining text value to display if true and if false

5. Click Enter, because the if-test is True, then the text displayed will be the first text.

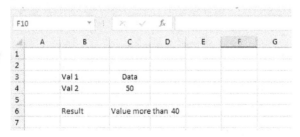

Pic 1.108 Second text displayed because the if-test equal FALSE

6. If the test value changed, so the if-test valued False, the first text will be displayed.

	A	B	C	D	E	F	G
1							
2							
3		Val 1	Data				
4		Val 2	30				
5							
6		Result	Value less than 40				
7							
8							
9							
10							

Pic 1.109 If C4's value updated, the if-test will be False

1.6 Working with Data

When dealing with data, there are many techniques to make data editing easier. You will learn some of them here.

1.6.1 Freeze Panes

If the data very broad and cannot display in a single window, you could freeze some panel so that you can slide some data, while other data were frozen.

Here is the example:

1. There is a full data we want to freeze.

Pic 1.110 Wide data we want to freeze

56

2. Click the cell which we want to freeze. This feature is basically below the data column header, and row header, or the column or row that freeze (stay unscrolled).

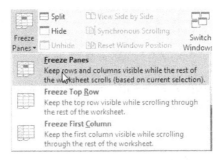

Pic 1.111 Click on the cell that will act as

3. Click **View** tab on the ribbon, then click **Freeze Panes > Freeze Panes**.

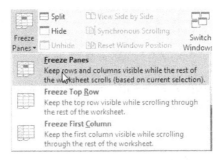

Pic 1.112 Freeze Panes menu to activate Freeze Panes

4. After the freeze, if you slide horizontally the data will be scrolled horizontally, but the left column stays unscrolled.

	A	L	M	N	O
1	Tgl	September	Oktober		
2	1	Rp 33.000,00	Rp 17.000,00		
3	2	Rp 33.000,00	Rp 30.000,00		
4	3	Rp 33.000,00	Rp 17.000,00		
5	4	Rp 33.000,00	Rp 30.000,00		
6	5	Rp 33.000,00	Rp 17.000,00		
7	6	Rp 33.000,00	Rp 30.000,00		
8	7	Rp 33.000,00	Rp 17.000,00		
9	8	Rp 33.000,00	Rp 30.000,00		
10	9	Rp 33.000,00	Rp 30.000,00		
11	10	Rp 33.000,00	Rp 17.000,00		
12	11	Rp 33.000,00	Rp 30.000,00		
13	12	Rp 33.000,00	Rp 17.000,00		
14	13	Rp 33.000,00	Rp 30.000,00		
15	14	Rp 33.000,00	Rp 17.000,00		
16	15	Rp 33.000,00	Rp 30.000,00		
17	16	Rp 33.000,00	Rp 17.000,00		
18	17	Rp 33.000,00	Rp 30.000,00		
19	18	Rp 33.000,00	Rp 17.000,00		
20	19	Rp 33.000,00	Rp 30.000,00		
21	20	Rp 33.000,00	Rp 17.000,00		
22	21	Rp 33.000,00	Rp 30.000,00		

Pic 1.113 Column B, C scrolled

5. If the data scrolled vertically, the rows below the header row would scroll above.

	A	L	M	N	O
1	Tgl	September	Oktober		
22	21	Rp 33.000,00	Rp 30.000,00		
23	22	Rp 33.000,00	Rp 17.000,00		
24	23	Rp 33.000,00	Rp 30.000,00		
25	24	Rp 33.000,00	Rp 30.000,00		
26	25	Rp 33.000,00	Rp 17.000,00		
27	26	Rp 33.000,00	Rp 30.000,00		
28	27	Rp 33.000,00	Rp 17.000,00		
29	28	Rp 33.000,00	Rp 30.000,00		
30	29	Rp 33.000,00	Rp 17.000,00		
31	30	Rp 33.000,00	Rp 30.000,00		
32	31	Rp 33.000,00	Rp 17.000,00		
33	Jml Total				
34					
35					
36					

Pic 1.114 Rows scrolled while the header does not

6. To remove the Freeze Panes effect, click View tab, then click **Freeze panes > Unfreeze Panes**.

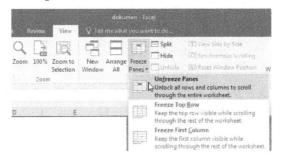

Pic 1.115 Click for Panes > Unfreeze Panes

7. After unfrozen, the data will fully back appear.

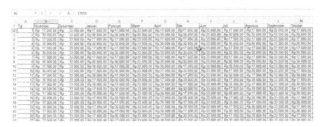

Pic 1.116 The data appear full after unfreeze

1.6.2 Sorting Data

A numeric and alphanumeric data can be sorted using certain criteria. Here is the example:

1. For example, there is a data of worker.

	A	B	C	D	E
1	Name	Department	Age		
2	Jonny	Marketing	54		
3	Jokowi	Marketing	24		
4	Jean	Jig & Fixtures	40		
5	Andrew	Assembly	52		
6	Raghib	Welding	19		
7	Errick	Welding	29		
8	Susilo	Welding	29		
9	Jeff	Jig & Fixtures	39		
10	Stephen	Marketing	19		
11					
12					
13					

Pic 1.117 Data of worker

2. For numerical value, you can sort from small to large by selecting the cells, then click **Sort > Sort Smallest to Largest**. This will sort the numeric data from smallest to largest

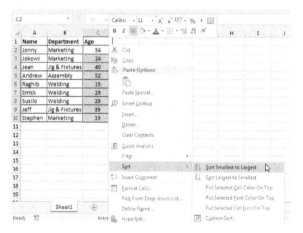

Pic 1.118 Sort Smallest to largest

3. The data on the column will be sorted automatically, while the data in another column will be adjusted too because I select **Expand the selection**.

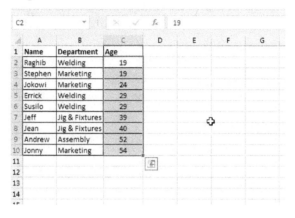

Pic 1.119 Result of sorting

1.6.4 Filtering Data

Filtering data will make excel only display data that match the criteria. Here is an example:

1. Click on the column to be filtered.

2. Right click and choose **Filter > Filter by selected cell's value**.

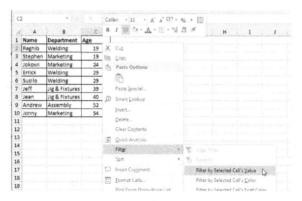

Pic 1.120 Filtering by selected cell's value

3. All of the table content will be empty. This is happening because everything is filtered.

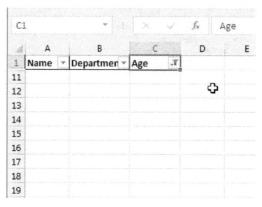

Pic 1.121 Table content empty because everything is filtered

4. Click on filter icon, then choose Select All to display all data.

Pic 1.122 Select all to display everything

5. All content of the table will be displayed.

Pic 1.123 All content displayed

6. You can also filter some data to be displayed by checking the value you want to show.

Pic 1.124 Checking on particular value to display

7. The data selected will be displayed.

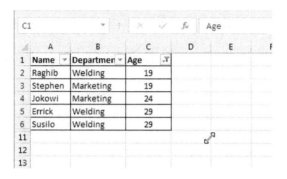

Pic 1.125 Data selected will be displayed

8. You can also create criteria for filtering. For example to display data which has more than a value, right-click on the column, then **Number Filters > Greater Than**.

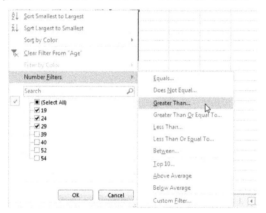

Pic 1.126 Number Filters > Greater than

9. Enter the value for filtering, for example, 50 on **Is bigger than** a text box. This value will only display values greater than 50.

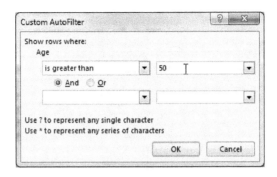

Pic 1.127 Entering criteria for filtering

10. Data that will be displayed will be the data with value > 50.

Pic 1.128 Data presented will have data value > 50

11. To remove filtering, click **Sort & Filter > Filter**. The filtering will be deleted.

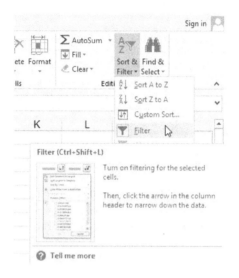

1.6.5 Table

A regular data in excel can be formatted as Excel table. This feature will make creating chart and table's data manipulation easier. Here is how you can create regular data as a table:

1. Choose all cells you want to incorporate into a table.

| C10 | ▾ | : | × | ✓ | fx | 54 |

▲	A	B	C	D
1	Name	Department	Age	
2	Raghib	Welding	19	
3	Stephen	Marketing	19	
4	Jokowi	Marketing	24	
5	Errick	Welding	29	
6	Susilo	Welding	29	
7	Jeff	Jig & Fixtures	39	
8	Jean	Jig & Fixtures	40	
9	Andrew	Assembly	52	
10	Jonny	Marketing	54	
11				
12				
13				
14				

Pic 1.130 Selecting Range to be incorporated into an excel table

2. Click Format as Table and choose the table style format you want.

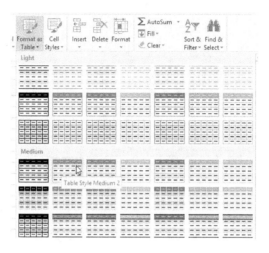

Pic 1.131 Select table style format

3. The range will be chosen, you can see dotted line encircling your table. If the table has a header, check **My table has headers**.

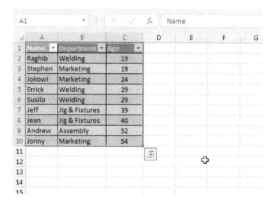

Pic 1.132 Click OK to create table from range selected

4. Click OK, the range you selected will become an excel table. When the data became a table, a filtering arrow will appear on the header.

Pic 1.133 Filtering arrow on each column's header

5. When you select a cell outside, the range still formatted as a table. A table can also be selected by inserting table's name on **Name** text box.

Pic 1.134 Ranges already formatted as table

1.7   Chart & Pivot Table

The chart is a visual representation of data in Excel's worksheet. The chart makes regular user can understand data easier than just reading numeric data. Excel support many charts as follows:

Chapter 1 Pie chart: Used to show percentage. This will tell how much a slice of the data value compared to other slice and overall values of the cell.

Chapter 2 Column chart: Used to compare between items. Each column shows a value of data.

Chapter 3 Bar chart: similar with column chart, just located horizontally and not vertically like a column.

Chapter 4 Line chart: Nice to show the trend of data, from time to time.

Chart sometimes called as graphic. Besides charts above, there are lots of another chart type in excel.

1.7.1 Creating Chart

To create a graph, you should do three things:

First inserting data, no matter what type of chart you want to create, you should enter data to the worksheet.

When entering data into a worksheet, please consider some pieces of information below:

1. Don't let empty cell or row/column between data. If there is an empty row or column between data, this will make Excel Chart Wizard not efficient. Hence will make creating chart harder, you have to select data manually.

2. If you can, insert data in column style. You just type the data name in the header, and then the data series for that header below   the   header   name   in   one   column.

Second is choosing data.

	A	B	C	D
	10R x 2C ▾		*fx* Location	
1	Average Precipitation for World Cities (mm)			
2				
3	Location	January	April	July
4	Acapulco	10	5	208
5	Amsterdam	69	53	76
6	Anchorage	17	13	42.5
7	Dallas	48	87.5	62
8	Glasgow	110	50	61
9	Madrid	39	48	11
10	New York	99	100	115
11	Tokyo	101	121	189
12	Toronto	55.2	65.4	71
13				

Drag with mouse

Pic 1.135 Choosing data

To pick data, you have to:

1. Click from the top-left of the data

2. Drag pointer across data, so every cell should be selected.

The third step is by choosing what methods were taken, using chart wizard or manual.

1.7.2 Creating Column Chart

To show how to create a chart, I will demonstrate how to build column chart. By following this example, you can create another type of charts easily, because basically, all chart is same.

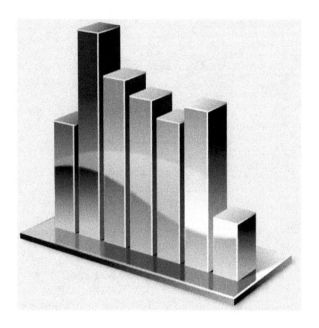

Pic 1.136 Column chart

Look at the example below:

1. The data for this example like this:

Salesman	Total Sales
Jimmi	10000
Joan	12000
Tri	18000
Tony	11000
Jerry	9000

2. Select all the table, including the text in the header.

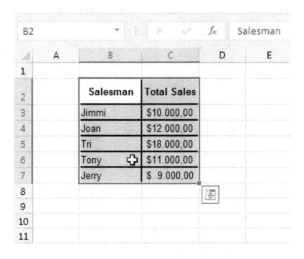

Pic 1.137 Selecting all table component

3. Click Insert Chart, because the chart we want to create is column chart, choose Column.

Pic 1.138 Creating Column

4. Click on one sub-type of the column type.

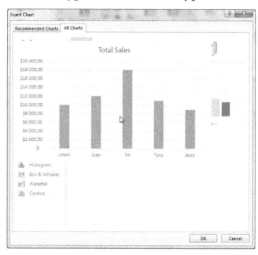

Pic 1.139 Choosing sub-type from Column chart

5. A table will be created automatically.

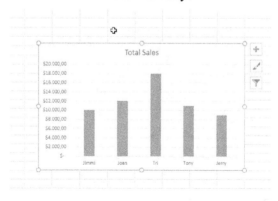

Pic 1.140 Column table created automatically

6. You can also create a table by clicking Insert > Column then choose sub-type of the column table you want to create.

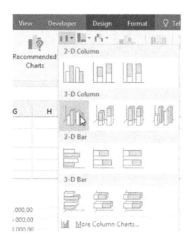

Pic 1.141 Choosing column table type

7. A new table will be created.

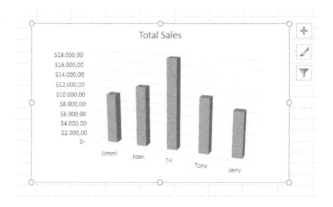

Pic 1.142 New table created

8. The table already created can be customized, for example, the horizontal lines can be deleted by click on one of the lines, then right click and click **Delete**.

Pic 1.143 Using Delete menu to delete horizontal lines

9. The horizontal line will be deleted from the table.

Pic 1.144 Horizontal line deleted from table

10. To format certain columns on the chart, right click and choose **Format** **Data** **Point**.

Pic 1.145 Menu Format Data Point to format columns on the chart

11. The first tab is Series options. You can change the depth and width properties of the series options. Select by changing the depth and width.

Pic 1.146 Series options

12. Fill tab is used to manage colors, pattern, or picture to fill the   columns.

Pic 1.147 Format Data Point

13. After the column is changed, the column will have a different style.

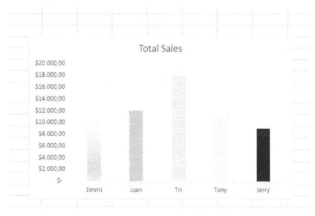

Pic 1.148 Column have different styles

14. In Border color, you can define what type of border for the columns.

Pic 1.149 Border Color

15. The   columns   will   be   bordered.

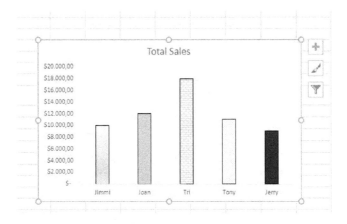

Pic 1.150 Columns after bordered

16. In Shadow, you can give shadows for the data points/columns.

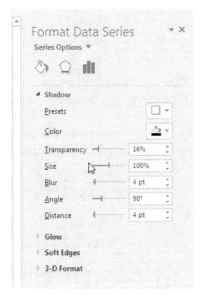

Pic 1.151 Configuring Shadow

---

17. In 3D Format, you can configure the 3D style for data points/columns.

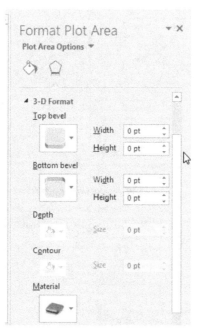

Pic 1.152 Configuring 3D-format for data points

18. The format of the columns or data points from the chart will be different from the default condition.

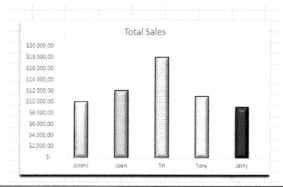

19. To change the title of the chart, you can click the title box.

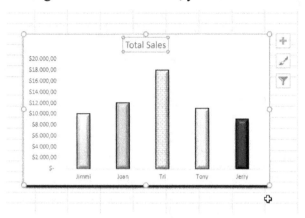

Pic 1.154 Clicking the title box to change chart's title

20. Type the new text for the title.

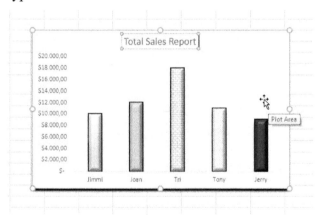

Pic 1.155 Typing new text for title

21. To see data source, right-click and choose **Select data**.

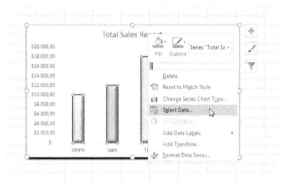

Pic 1.156 Menu to Select Data

22. You can see series of data used as legend entries and axis labels.

Pic 1.157 Data source

23. When Data Source window opened, you can see which column act as legend entries and Axis labels.

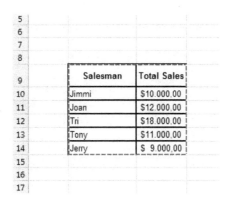

	Salesman	Total Sales
10	Jimmi	$10.000,00
11	Joan	$12.000,00
12	Tri	$18.000,00
13	Tony	$11.000,00
14	Jerry	$ 9.000,00

Pic 1.158 Data source

24. You can change the type of chart to a different kind of column by clicking **Column > Other Column Type**.

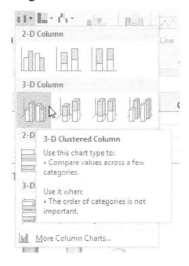

Pic 1.159 Column > Other Column Type

1.7.3 Pivot Table

A table can be pivoted to create a pivot table. This table will help you to see information more clearly. You can see some aggregated data which it cannot be seen using the standard table. Here is how to create pivot table:

1. Click on **Insert > Pivot table**.

Pic 1.160 Click Insert > PivotTable

2. Choose the range that has data to make the table and click **OK**.

Pic 1.161 Choosing range to create pivot table

3. Pivot table box appeared, but you haven't seen any columns entered.

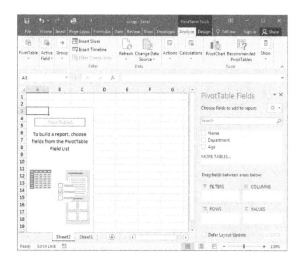

Pic 1.162 Pivot table entered

4. For example, if we want to know the average age for each department, you can enter pic below:

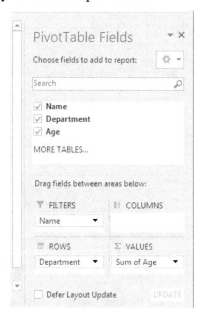

5. You can see SUM for age.

	A	B	C	D
1	Name	(All) ▼		
2				
3	Row Labels ▼	Sum of Age		
4	Assembly	52		
5	Jig & Fixtures	79		
6	Marketing	97		
7	Welding	77		
8	**Grand Total**	**305**		
9				

Pic 1.164 Pivot table for sum for Age

6. To change the aggregation type, click on Sum of Age and click **Value Field Settings**.

Pic 1.165 Choosing Value Field Settings

7. Choose **Summarize type** to **Average**.

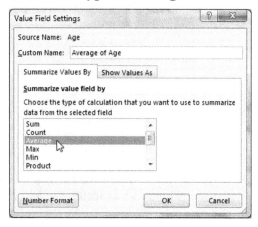

Pic 1.167 Choosing Summarize Type to Average

8. You can see the average age of each department.

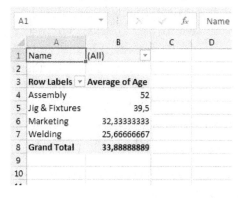

Pic 1.168 Average age per department

Chapter 2 LEARNING ACCESS

Microsoft Access is an RDBMS software, used to manage data in a database. RDBMS means relational database management system. This app belongs to Microsoft Office app. This app has an intuitive user interface and nice GUI to make managing data in database easier.

2.1   Introducing to MS Access

Microsoft Access can manage data that are saved in many formats, such as Microsoft Access, Microsoft Jet Database Engine, Microsoft SQL Server, Oracle Database, and other database containers that support ODBC standard.

Developer/Programmer can use MS Access to develop complex or simple application software. Access also supports object-oriented programming, although cannot be classified as a full OOP programming IDE.

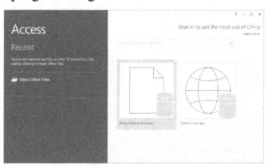

2.1.1 MS Access Objects

Database mainly used to store database efficiently, where the data can be selected, updated, or deleted. To accommodate that function, the database in MS Access has several objects:

o	Objects	Function
.	Table	A place to save data.
.	Query	Language or syntax to manipulate data or database.
.	Form	An interface to manage data/information in the database using desktop user interface. This feature makes interaction to data easier and useful in avoiding errors
.	Report	Object to display and print data/information as a report. Usually, it is printed on paper.

2.1.2 Opening and Closing MS Access

To run MS Access, you can do steps below:
1. The fastest way is by clicking Windows + R on your keyboard then type "msaccess" command and click **OK.**

Pic 2.2 Entering "msaccess" command in MS access

2. The initial MS Access window looks like this:

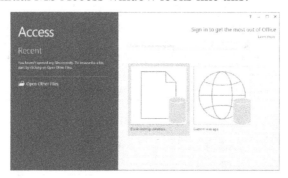

Pic 2.3 Initial MS Access 2016 window

3. To close this window, click **File > Close**:

Pic 2.4 File > Exit menu to close MS Access window

4. You can also close MS Access by clicking cross [X] sign on the top right of the window, or by clicking **ALT + F4** shortcut on your keyboard.

2.1.3 MS Access' Interfaces

When opening MS Access interface, there are two options. The first option is by creating a blank database and the Second is creating a database based on individual templates.

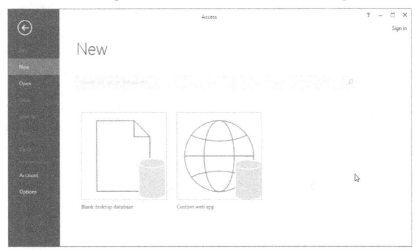

Pic 2.6 Available Templates

If you want to create a database based on models, find the template by inserting the keyword in **Search for online templates** textbox. You can scroll down the window to find lots of templates here.

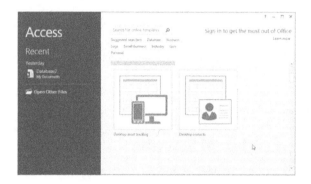

Pic 2.7 Office.com Templates

After the keyword inserted, and you click Enter on your keyboard, all templates related to the keyword entered will be displayed.

Pic 2.8 Search result on templates keyword

To create a database based on a template, just click the template. The detail of the template will be displayed. You can enter database name you want to create in **File name** text box. Then clicks **Create** button to create the database.

Pic 2.9 The detail of template

The template chosen will be downloaded and created.

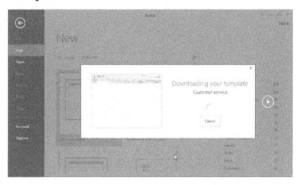

Pic 2.10 Template is downloaded to create new database based on that template

The newly created database will already have a structure:

Pic 2.11 Newly created database already has structure

2.1.4 Configuring MS Access Options

To be able to work efficiently, you should configure MS access options to suits your need. Click **File > Options** to configure app's options.

Pic 2.12 Click on File > Options to start configuring apps

In **General** tab, you can activate Live preview, activate Clear type to enhance the text's appearance on MS Access. You can also change the color scheme of MS Access window by choosing in combo box Office Theme.

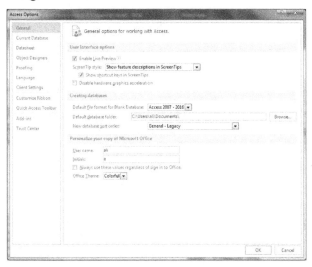

Pic 2.13 Tab General to configure general options of MS Access

In **the current database**, you can set up options on how database behave. Such as the application title, application icons, you can set whether the picture, navigation activated or not.

Pic 2.14 Current Database tab

In Datasheet tab, you can configure the Gridlines and cell effects, and you can set up font size, font weight, and font style.

Pic 2.15 Configuring Gridlines and Fonts

In **Object Designers** tab, you can configure options for object creation, such as defining default object type, you can also set default field text and standard field size.

In Query Design, you can define option when creating a query, such as whether you want to display table name, table field, etc. In Form/report design view, you can define the options when creating form or report.

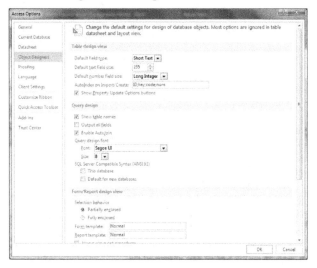

Pic 2.16 Object Designer

In Proofing, you can set proofing options for MS Access, such as AutoCorrect Options, and Spelling correction. You can define the dictionary language as the base for language proofing.

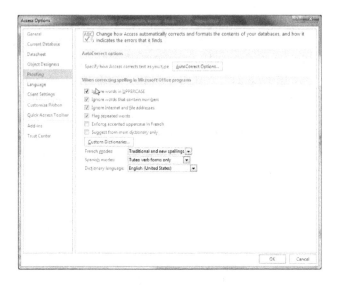

Pic 2.17 Language Proofing Tab

In Language, you can see the libraries for editing function. This feature depends on your computer settings. Because I use an Indonesia user interface, the default Is Indonesian and English.

To add a language, choose the language in combo box Add Additional editing language, and click Add. In the beginning, the library for the language status was "Not installed." Click that link.

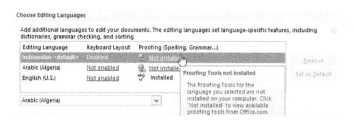

Pic 2.19 Click Not installed to open the language package

A download page will emerge from Office.microsoft.com. Just click the download link to download proofing package for that language. On Client settings, you can configure editing aspects of MS Access, such as, how to move after entering, confirmation, behavior, etc.

In Customize Ribbon, you can choose to customize the ribbon, by adding or removing commands and text from existing commands in the ribbon.

Pic 2.21 Customize Ribbon tab

In **Quick Access Toolbar**, you can add button in Quick Access toolbar. This feature is on the top left of your window.

Pic 2.22 Customizing quick access toolbar

In Add-Ins, you can add-in software to add features on your MS Access programs.

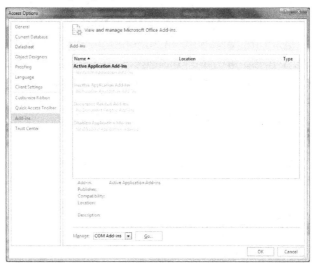

Pic 2.23 Add-ins tab

In Trust Center, you can configure options to protect your documents.

Pic 2.24 Trust Center

2.1.5 Create, Save and Open Database

Before doing database manipulation, you should create a database. On the previous example, you have created a database from a template. Now you should create a blank database.

You can follow the tutorial below:

1. Click on tab File.

2. To create a blank database, click Blank database in **the Available   template.**

Pic 2.25 Adding Blank database

3. Fill the name for the database in File name text box, then click **Create**.

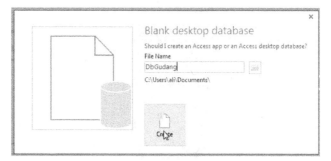

Pic 2.26 Click Create to create a file name

4. When opened, you can see new table interface. But the table hasn't yet created because the table hasn't been saved.

Pic 2.27 Blank database on MS Access window

5. To save database file, click **File > Save**.

Pic 2.28 File > Save to save MS Access database file

6. To save to another type of database file, click **File > Save As > Save Database As.**

Pic 2.29 File > Save As > Save database as

7. Enter the new file name in Save As, click **Save**.

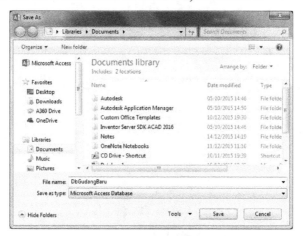

Pic 2.30 Naming the file and click Save

8. If database editing already finished, click **File > Close database** to close the database.

Pic 2.31 File > Close database to close the database

9. To open the database file, click **File > Open**.

Pic 2.32 Click on File > Open

10. Choose   the   database   file   you   want   to   open.

Pic 2.33 Choosing Access database file to open

11. The file will be opened, and you can manipulate your database. When a file is opened, you can see the title bar will display file name.

Pic 2.34 File already opened, you can see the name of the archive in title bar

2.1.6 Understanding Buttons in Ribbon

In Ribbon, there are some buttons you can use to manipulate the database. The first is Home tab that contains buttons to edit and format database.

Pic 2.35 Tab Home di Ribbon

Some buttons in Home tab are:

1. View : changing the view of objects from many angles. For example, modify the table to view or input data.

2. Paste : pasting file or object from clipboard collected from copy or cut operation.

3. ✂ Cut : cutting object. Object cut-ted will disappear and stays on the clipboard, that can be pasted using Paste button.

4. 📋 Copy : copying object. Object copied will stays on the clipboard.

5. ✏ Format Painter : copying formatting from one place (for example: text) to another.

6. Filter : filtering data.

7. ↓ Ascending : showing data using ascending order, from smallest to largest. From a to z.

8. $\overset{A}{Z}\downarrow$ Descending : showing data using descending order, from largest to smallest, from z to a.

9. Remove Sort : removing sorting effect.

10. Selection ˅ : Filtering selection

11. Advanced ˅ : doing advanced filtering

12. Refresh All ˅ : refresh everything

13. New : create a new record on the table.

14. Save : save new record in table

15. Delete ˅ : deleting the record.

16. Σ Totals : Summing the total.

17. Spelling : check the spelling.

18. Find : find certain texts.

19. Calibri (Detail) ˅ : setting the font to a particular style.

20. 11 ˅ : configuring font size.

21. B : implementing bold style to selected texts.

22. I : applying the italic style to selected texts.

23. U : Right-click underline to selected texts.

24. A ˅ : select text's color.

25. : select cell color.

26.  : select the inline alignment, whether left, right or center.

The second tab is **Create**. There are many buttons to accommodate objects creation in MS Access.

Pic 2.36 Tab Create

Some buttons in Create tab are:

1. Templates : create an object based on the available template.

2. Table : creating a table.

3. Design : Switching to table design.

4. Lists ▾ : Managing share point lists.

5. Wizard : Creating query using a wizard.

6. Design: Creating query using design interface.

7.   :   creating   a   new   form.

8. Form Design : Creating a form using design interface.

9. Blank Form : creating empty form.

10. Form Wizard : creating a new form of wizard.

11. Navigation ▾ : Adding navigation form.

12. More Forms ▾ : Adding more form.

13. Report : creating a report.

14. Report Design : creating a report using design view.

15. Blank Report : creating a new blank report.

16. Report Wizard : creating report using wizard

17. Labels : entering labels in a report.

18. Macro : creating a macro.

19. Module : creating macro for module

20. Class Module : creating a class module.

21.  Visual Basic : creating a visual basic module.

The third tab is External data tab. This tab is used to import and export data.

Pic 2.37 External data tab

Some of the buttons on External Data tab are:

1. Saved Imports : Displaying saved imports on a document.

2. Linked Table Manager : linking table from other data source.

3. Excel : importing from excel.

4. Access : importing data from MS Access.

5. ODBC Database : importing from ODBC data source.

6. Text File : importing from text files.

7. XML File : importing from an XML file.

8. More : importing from other files.

9. Saved Exports : Export a document.

10. Excel : Exporting data to excel file.

11. Text File : Exporting data to text file.

12. XML File : Exporting data to an XML file.

13. PDF or XPS : Exporting data to pdf or xps file.

14. E-mail : Exporting data to email file.

15. A Access : Exporting data to another access file.

16. W Word Merge : using word merge.

17. More ˅ : More options for exporting ms access data.

18. Create E-mail : Create an email with the Access document as an attachment.

19. Manage Replies : Managing reply.

The fourth tab in the ribbon is Database Tools. Here you can see many database related tools.

Pic 2.38 Database Tools tab in ribbon

Some buttons from this database tools tab are:

1. Compact and Repair Database Tools : Compacting and Repairing database.

2. Visual Basic : Opening VB window to do programming in Visual Basic.

3. Run Macro : Running macro.

4. Relationships : Opening relationship window that displays relations between database objects.

5. Object Dependencies : Displaying object dependencies.

6. Database Documenter : Open Database Documenter.

7. Analyze Performance : Analyze performance of objects.

8. Analyze Table : Analyzing table

9. ^{SQL} Server : Opening SQL Server window to manage remote SQL Server database.

10. ^{Access} Database : Managing access databases.

SharePoint

11. : Opening share point window to manage share point database.

Add-ins

12. : Opening add-ins window to add or remove add-ins.

Next tab is Formatting tab. The appearance of this tab depends on objects selected.

Pic 2.39 Formatting tabs that display objects connected to

2.2   Introduction to Object Table

A database has a table to save data. Without the table, there will be no query and form, because of query and form query or manipulate data from the table.

The table looks like spreadsheet form; it has rows and columns. Colum represents particular data type, while row represents data on an individual item. The row in table usually called   record.

Pic 2.40 Example of table, rows, and columns

2.2.1 Creating Table

The table is the place for saving data. To keep data efficiently, you should create table effectively.

Here is how to create a table in MS Access:
1. Open database, when there is no table, you can see the **All Access Objects** window empty.

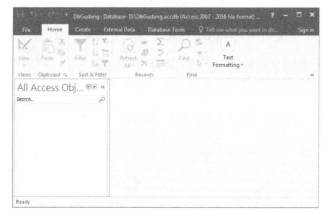

Pic 2.41 All Access Objects empty because no table has been created

2. Click on Create > Table to create a new table.

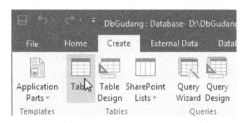

Pic 2.42 Click on Create > Table to create new tab

3. A new table named Table1 will emerge, and in the All Access Objects window, an icon will appear **Table1**. But this table hasn't yet created.

Pic 2.43 Table already created but have not yet saved.

4. Click CTRL + S to save the table. A Save As window emerge,   insert   the   table   name.

Pic 2.44 CTRL + S and inserting table's name

5. A table will be created, the name you entered on the textbox on the previous window will be the name of the table. You can see the table created on **All Access Objects > Tables**.

Pic 2.45 Table name already visible in All Access Objects

6. Start inserting content to table by changing to Design View by   clicking   **View**   **>**   **Design   View**.

Pic 2.46 Click on View > Design View

7. If you open the Design View, the default table will have one primary key with the field name ID, and data type AutoNumber.

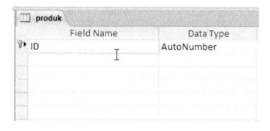

Pic 2.47 Default field

8. You can manipulate fields by inserting the identity, for example for **Products** table. We need barcodeNumber field.

Pic 2.48 Inserting field Barcode Number

9. Insert other fields as necessary. The bottom side of the user interface has the General tab which you can use to specify more advanced properties of the field.

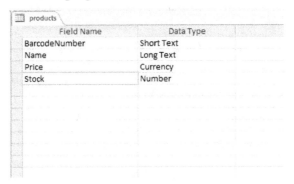

Pic 2.49 Inserting additional fields

10.   A table should have primary key ideally. The primary key is a field used as identity. Its value have to be unique, duplicate content is not allowed. To assign a field as primary key, right-click on the header of the row then choose **Primary   Key   menu.**

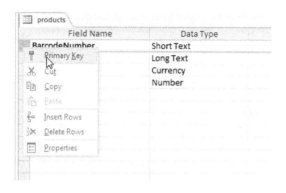

2.2.1.1 Editing Table Structure

When a table created, the structure of the table still can be edited again. For example, renaming certain fields, change data type fields, or delete/add certain fields. Here

1. For example, the **stock** field will be renamed to the **shelf**.

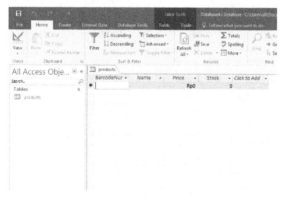

Pic 2.51 Initial table condition

2. Right-click on the table name, then click Design View menu to switch to Design View type.

Pic 2.52 Click Design view menu to open Design View

3. After the Design View created, you can click on the field name you want to rename.

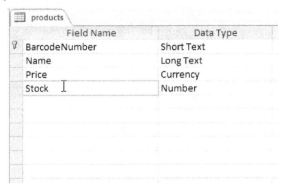

Pic 2.53 Click on field name to rename

4. Type the new name for the field. Then click CTRL + S to save   the   table.

Pic 2.54 Saving after renaming the field

2.2.1.2 Copying Tabel

An already created table can be copied to make another table with similar content. Here are steps to do:

1. Click on table's icon in **All Access Objects** window. Then click the **Home > Copy** button.

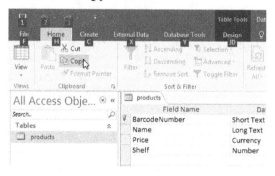

Pic 2.55 Click Home > Copy button to copy

2. Click on **Home > Paste** button to paste table object copied.

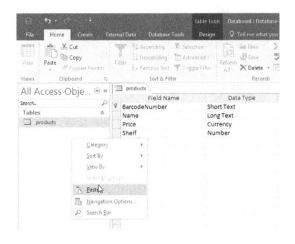

Pic 2.56 Click Home > Paste to paste table object

3. A window titled **Paste Table As** emerged, you can define the table copying option. For example, whether you want to copy the structure only, structure and data, or append data to the existing table.

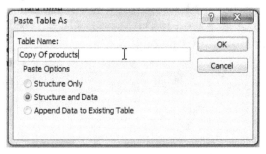

Pic 2.57 Paste Table As window

4. You can rename the table's name on Table Name text box. You can also define whether the structure or the structure & data added. Click OK process.

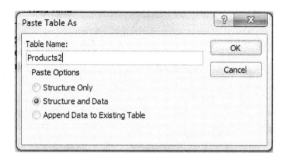

Pic 2.58 Rename table's name

5. The newly copied table will be available in **All Access Objects > Tables** window.

Pic 2.59 Table's name created from

6. If the newly created table opened, you can see the structure and the data are similar to the previous table.

Pic 2.60 Newly created table opened

2.2.1.3 Deleting Fields

Fields no longer needed can be deleted. Here is how to do it:

1. Right-click on the field's header you want to remove, then click **Delete Field**.

Pic 2.61 Delete Field menu to delete unused field

2. The deleted field will be removed permanently from the database.

Pic 2.62 Field will be deleted

2.2.1.4 Access Data Types

While creating a table, you already interacted with some data types. Here are details of some data types in MS Access:

1. Text: The most prevalent data type used. This data type can be used to alphanumeric needs. For example, name address, postcode, phone number. Microsoft Access can accommodate up to 255 chars for this data type. It has two variations, short text, and long text.

2. Memo: This is almost similar to Text, but can accommodate up to 64,000 chars. This data type rarely used because can not be sorted or indexed.

3. Number: This data type is used to save the numerical value that used on mathematical calculation. You don't use this data type for a phone number for example because phone number doesn't need to be calculated.

4. Date/Time: This data type is for saving date and time, you can use this data type for saving the birth date or buying time for a product.

5. Currency

This feature is for saving currency values. Although you can use Number for saving money until four decimal points.

6. AutoNumber: This is long integer value used automatically for each record added to the table. You don't have to add anything in this field, AutoNumber usually used to identify each record in a table.

7. Yes/No: This is to save boolean values yes or No.

8. OLE Object: This is rarely used, OLE object used to save the binary file, like image or audio files.

9. Hyperlink: This is for saving URLs to a specified address on the internet.

10. Attachment: You can use this data type to save a file or even some files in one single field. Attachment field exists since Access 2007. This field is more efficient than OLE object field.

When creating a table, you should ensure some checklist on table naming below:

1. Max length of the field name is 64 characters. Although you have to give descriptive name, make sure it's under 64 chars.

2. Field name may not contain (.), exclamation mark (!), single quotation mark/accent (`), or square brackets ([ ]).

3. Don't use space in field or table name. If you need to define space in the field name, use underscore (_) instead.

2.2.2 Deleting Table

The unneeded table can be deleted using steps below:

1. Close the table first, because the opened table can not be removed. Rith clicks on table's tab and clicks **Close** menu.

Pic 2.63 Closing table before deletion

2. Right-click on a table in All Access Object window, and click **Delete**.

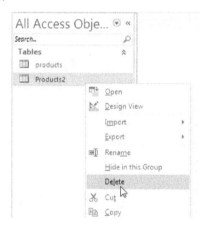

Pic 2.64 Delete menu to delete table

3. A confirmation window will appear, click **Yes**.

Pic 2.65 Confirmation to delete table

4. The table will disappear from **All Access Objects** window. This shows that the table already removed.

Pic 2.66 The Table deleted disappear from All Access Objects window

2.2.3 Inserting Data and Editing

The table is a place to save data after the table created, you can insert data and editing. Here is a tutorial to do that:

1. Open the table you want to insert your data into, Click on the top-left cell.

Pic 2.67 Put pointer on top-left cell in the first row

2. You can enter data by typing directly in the table. For certain field, you can enter using another input reader, such as barcode   reader.

Pic 2.68 Inserting data

3. To add new line/record. Click on the lowest row, and type just like the previous.

Pic 2.69 Inserting new record

4. While typing, you can see the pencil icon on the left. This icon means the data is still currently adding.

Pic 2.70 Pencil icon shows the data is still currently adding

5. Data in one row can be copied to another row. Just select the row heading on the left, then right click and click **Copy** menu.

Pic 2.71 Context menu to do Copy

6. Now, click on the row you want to and click **Paste**.

Pic 2.72 Paste the copied object from clipboard

7. After the paste, the text will be copied to the selected row.

Pic 2.73 Selected text after copied

8. For some occasion, when a primary key doesn't let you have identical value in one field, you can edit the copied text with other value.

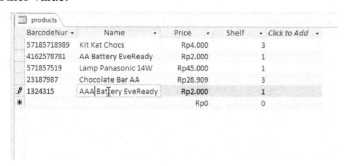

Pic 2.74 Editing text because primary key restriction

9. To delete a record, right-click on record and click **Delete record** menu.

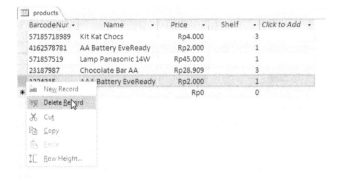

Pic 2.75 Delete Record menu

10. Confirmation window emerges, you are asked whether "You are about to delete one record(s)". Click **Yes** to remove the record permanently.

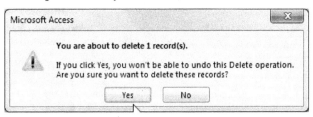

Pic 2.76 Record Deletion confirmation

11. The selected record will be deleted and removed permanently from the table.

2.2.3.1 Sorting Data

Sorting feature in a table can be beneficial. Here is how to do data sorting in MS Access table:

1. Right-click on the field, then choose the sorting type, for example, **Sort smallest to largest** to make the data in the table displayed based on smallest value to largest value.

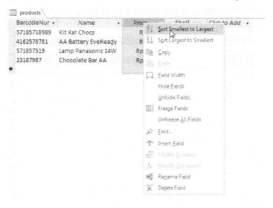

Pic 2.78 Sorting from smallest to largest

2. The data will be sorted accordingly:

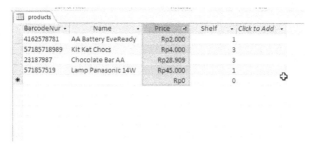

Pic 2.79 The data sorted from smallest to largest on Price field

3. The sorting in a table is not restricted to one field only. You can also do sorting on multi-fields for example after sorting the Price field. You can sort the Name field from Z to A by

right-click on the field, and click **Sort z to a**.

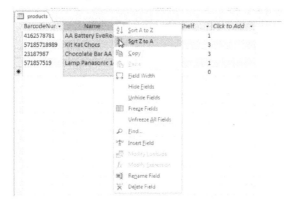

Pic 2.80 Sorting from Z to A

4. The data will be sorted accordingly, in price field first, then the Name field.

Pic 2.81 Sorting data based on price and name

5. To remove the sorting effect, click on **Home > Remove Sort** in **Sort & Filter** box.

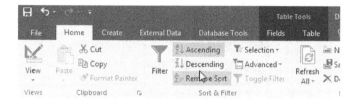

Pic 2.82 Remove sort remove sorting based on alphabet

6. After the sorting effect removed, the table will have the initial order.

Pic 2.83 Data with the initial order

2.2.3.2 Configuring Row Height

Row height can be configured just like in excel. Here is the tutorial:

1. Select row in the table and right-click then click **Row height** menu.

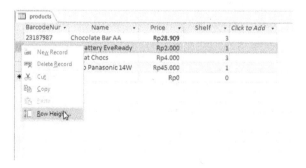

Pic 2.84 Row height

2. A Row Height window appears like this:

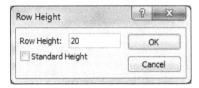

Pic 2.85 Configuring Row height

3. Enter row height you want for example 20 and click **OK**.

Pic 2.86 Row height after 20 pixels

4. To revert to initial size, right-click on Row height, and check Standard height text box. This action will alter the row height to 14.25.

Pic 2.87 Row height reverted

5. Row height will be reverted to the initial condition.

Pic 2.88 Row height will be reverted to initial condition

6. You can perform a filter on the data by right-clicking on the field then check on values you want to display.

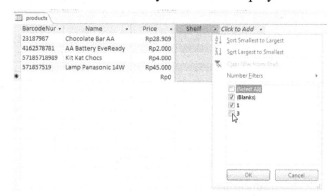

Pic 2.89 Check on values you want to display

7. Data will be filtered and the values checked will be shown.

Pic 2.90 Table filtered

8. To remove filtering effect, check on **Home > Toggle Filter** in Sort & Filter effect.

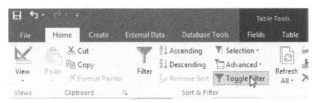

Pic 2.91 Check on Toggle Filter to remove filtering

9. The data displayed will revert to initial condition.

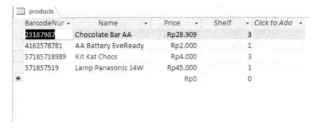

Pic 2.92 All data shown after filtering effect removed

2.3 Data Queries

Data without analysis is only a bunch of numbers and texts. But if you analyze the data, the data can be extracted as information. In Access, you should create a query to analyze the data from tables.

2.3.1 Access Queries

To analyze data, you have to retrieve data from the table. That is what the query used for. The query will extract data from the data source (table) and only display the data that matched the query created, or you can say the query result.

2.3.2 Select Query

To grab data from a table, use **SELECT** query. This query will extract data based on criteria provided. Access has GUI feature to make data query easier. You can use Query Design or query grid.

In Query Design, components like tables, views, and columns represented visually, this makes the query as easy as arranging puzzle. Here is an example of how to create a query using GUI in Access:

1. Click on **Create > Query Design**.

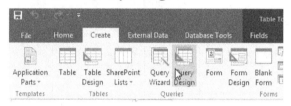

Pic 2.93 Click Create > Query Design to open Query Design window

2. Choose the table as a data source in Show Table window.

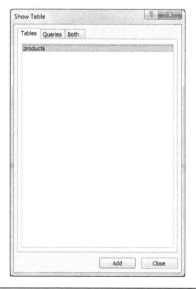

3. Tables selected will be inserted in the query window.

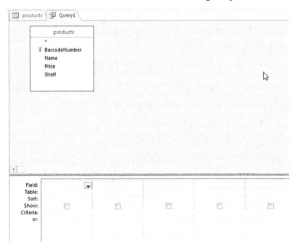

Pic 2.95 Tables added in query window

4. To create a select query, click **Design > Select** on Query Type.

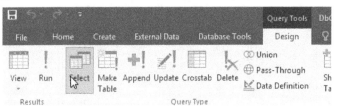

Pic 2.96 Click on Design > Select to create SELECT query

5. Choose   fields   you   want   to   insert.

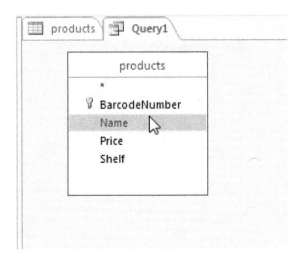

Pic 2.97 Choosing fields to insert

6. Fields added will appear on the bottom part of query window.

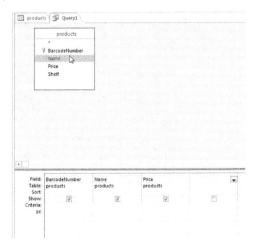

Pic 2.98 One field added

7. You can run the query by clicking a **Design > Run** (!) button.

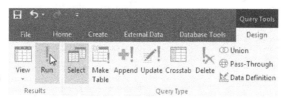

Pic 2.99 Running the query by clicking Design > Run

8. The query will display all data from table using the query you created.

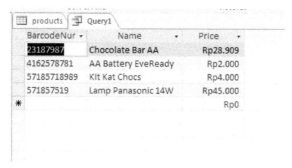

Pic 2.100 Query display data from table

9. To see the SQL statement (codes behind the query), right-click on the query and click **SQL view** menu. Or you can click **View > SQL View** in Access' toolbar.

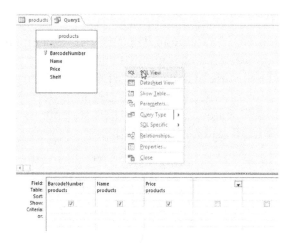

Pic 2.101 Menu to open SQL view

10. You can see the SQL SELECT statement created visually

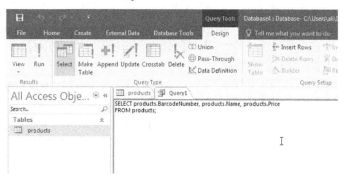

Pic 2.102 SQL Statement texts

2.3.3 SQL SELECT

When you create Select query above, basically, you are creating SQL SELECT statement visually. To enable you to create more SELECT query efficiently, you should understand the meaning of SQL SELECT statement.

The SELECT statement or SQL SELECT statement is the most popular SQL statement. The SELECT statement used to get/extract data from tables in the database.

You can decide what pieces of information taken from some areas, from what tables, you can also define the logics of the SELECT statement by WHERE statement. The syntax of SQL SELECT statement is like this:

```
SELECT column_list FROM table_names
[WHERE clause]
[GROUP BY clause]
[HAVING clause]
[ORDER BY clause];
```

Table_names are the name of tables you want to extract the data.

Column_list is the fields to display.

Another clause is optional.

In SQL SELECT, only SELECT and FROM are mandatory, other clauses like WHERE, ORDER BY, GROUP BY, HAVING are optional.

2.3.4 Sorting and Using Criteria in Select

SELECT statement can be classified using some criteria. For example, if you want the Select query result sorted ascending by name field, then you can choose sort Ascending in Name field.

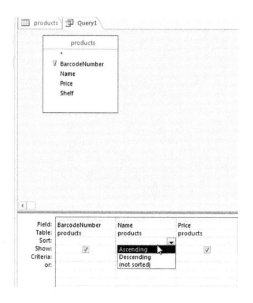

Pic 2.103 Choosing Sort as Ascending

If the query executed, the data will be sorted ascending from a to z.

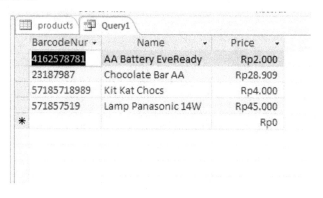

Pic 2.104 Query result sorted ascending

You also add other criteria by using the boolean operator for example, AND. Imagine if you want the data sorted by

Name Field, and the Price above 2500 then use > 2500 in criteria.

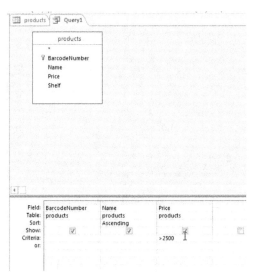

Pic 2.105 Adding criteria in Price field

If the query executed, you can see the rules affects the data selected by the query.

Pic 2.106 The criteria will affect the data selected by the query

You can make more than one criteria, for example, Price > 25 and Name starts with g by entering > "g" on field Name's criteria.

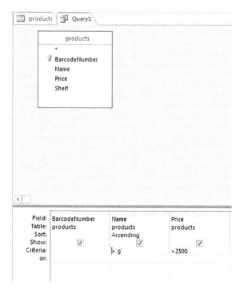

Pic 2.107 Using more than one criteria

If query executed, the rules will affect the data selected.

Pic 2.108 Query result after two criteria implemented

If you want to find exact data, you can use equal sign and enter the data you want to find in criteria row.

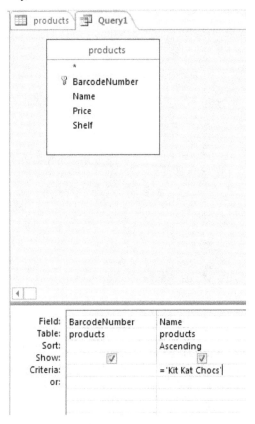

Pic 2.109 Finding exact text

When query executed, the correct result will be displayed.

Pic 2.110 Exact result will be displayed

To save the query, click on CTRL + S on the keyboard, enter the name of the query.

Pic 2.111 Entering name for the Query

In All Access Objects window, you can see the new query already saved.

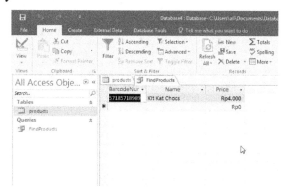

Pic 2.112 All Access objects display new query selected

2.3.5 Query Operators

The query can use more than one criteria using operators. Operators make combining boolean value on criteria easier. Here are some operators can be used in query:

1. Arithmetical operators: Access can use arithmetical operators such as =, +, -, *, /, >, <.

2. Or: This operator will return True if at least one of the criteria is True.

3. Between: This operator will test certain range, for example testing whether data between value A and value B or not?

4. Like: This operator will test string expression whether this string will fit with a certain pattern or not. For example, you can filter record with Name similar to certain text.

5. In: Similar to **OR**, to evaluate all record according to value in the argument. This syntax is very important if you have lots of criteria to evaluate.

6. Not: This is the reciprocal of In, NOT will filter all record that is complementary to all arguments in ( ).

7. Is Null: IS NULL will filter all record in the database that has a null value.

***

ABOUT THE AUTHOR

Ali Akbar is an IT Author who has more than ten years of experience in the architecture and has been using IT for more than 15 years. He has worked on design projects ranging from department store to transportation systems to the Semarang project. He is the all-time best-selling IT author and was cited as favorite IT author. Zico P. Putra is a senior engineering technician, IT consultant, author, & trainer with ten years of experience in several design fields. He continues his Ph.D. in the Queen Mary University of London. Find out more at https://www.amazon.com/dp/1521133646

CAN I ASK A FAVOUR?

If you enjoyed this book, found it useful or otherwise then I would appreciate it if you would post a short review on Amazon. I do read all the reviews personally so that I can continually write what people are wanting.

If you would like to leave a review, then please visit the link below:

https://www.amazon.com/dp/B0722FJ59B

Thanks for your support!

www.ingramcontent.com/pod-product-compliance
Lightning Source LLC
LaVergne TN
LVHW022318060326
832902LV00020B/3546